to share with your children

MAUREEN MILLER

ARGUS COMMUNICATIONS A Division of **DLM** Inc.
Niles, Illinois 60648

Acknowledgments

From *Man's Search for Himself* by Rollo May. Copyright © 1953 by W. W. Norton. Used by permission.

From *The Sane Society* by Erich Fromm. Copyright © 1955 Holt, Rinehart & Winston.

From *Understanding Your Child from Birth to Three: A Guide to Your Child's Psychological Development*, by Joseph Church. Copyright © 1975 by Random House. Used by permission.

From *Understanding Fear in Ourselves and in Others* by Bonaro Overstreet. Copyright © 1971. Harper and Row.

From *Your Child's Self-Esteem* by Dorothy Corkille Briggs. Copyright © 1970 by Dorothy Corkille Briggs. Reprinted by permission of Doubleday & Company, Inc.

From *The Secret of Staying in Love* by John Powell. Copyright © Argus Communications 1974.

From *How to be Your Own Best Friend* by Mildred Newman and Bernard Berkowitz. Copyright © 1973 by Random House. Used by permission.

Excerpted from *Opening*, by Bob Samples and Bob Wohlford, copyright © 1975, by permission of Addison-Wesley Publishing Company, Inc., Reading, Mass.

From *Making Contact* by Virginia Satir. Copyright © 1976 by Virginia Satir. Reprinted with permission of the publisher, Celestial Arts, Millbrae, CA 94030.

From *The Uses of Enchantment: The Meaning and Importance of Fairy Tales*, by Bruno Bettelheim. Copyright ©1976 by Alfred A. Knopf. Used by permission.

From *To Hallow This Life* by Martin Buber. Copyright © Harper and Row.

From *The Divine Milieu: An Essay on the Interior Life*, by Pierre Teilhard de Chardin. Copyright © 1960. Harper and Row.

From *Notes to Myself* by Hugh Prather, © 1970 Real People Press.

From *Schools Without Failure* by William Glasser. Copyright © 1969. Harper and Row.

From *On Caring* by Milton Mayeroff. Copyright © 1970. Harper and Row.

From "The Child Meets the World," by Antonia Wenkart, in *Existential Child Therapy: The Child's Discovery of Himself*, edited by Clark Moustakas, © 1966 by Clark Moustakas, Basic Books, Inc., Publishers, New York.

From Thomas Merton, *Seeds of Contemplation*. Copyright © 1949 by Our Lady of Gethsemani Monastery. Reprinted by permission of New Directions.

From *Why Am I Afraid to Tell You Who I Am?* by John Powell. Copyright © Argus Communications 1969.

From *The Heart of Man* by Gerald Vann, O.P. Copyright © 1945 by Gerald Vann, O.P. Reprinted by permission of Doubleday & Company, Inc.

From "Play and Family Development" by Robert Strom. *Elementary School Journal*. © University of Chicago Press.

From *Reality Therapy* by William Glasser. Copyright © 1965. Harper and Row.

Cover Design by Gene Tarpey
Illustrations by Sharon Elzaurdia

First Edition

Printed in the United States of America.

ARGUS COMMUNICATIONS
7440 Natchez Avenue
Niles, Illinois 60648

International Standard Book Number 0-89505-018-8
Library of Congress Number 78-73335

0 9 8 7 6 5 4 3 2

This book is dedicated to
Tasha, Joshua, Justin, Jeremy Brey, and Jessica
Who celebrate Life.

When will we also teach them what they are?
We should say to each of them: Do you know
what you are? You are a marvel. You are
unique. In all of the world there is no other child
exactly like you. In the millions of years that
have passed, there has never been a child like
you. And look at your body—what a wonder it
is! Your legs, your arms, your cunning fingers,
the way you move! You may become a
Shakespeare, a Michelangelo, a Beethoven. You
have the capacity for anything. Yes, you are a
marvel. And when you grow up, can you then
harm another who is, like you, a marvel? You
must cherish one another. You must work—
we must all work—to make this world worthy
of its children.

Pablo Casals

Contents

Joy is the goal of life, for joy is the emotion which accompanies our fulfilling our natures as human beings. It is based on the experience of one's identity as a being of worth and dignity, who is able to affirm his being, if need be, against all other beings and the whole inorganic world.

Rollo May,
Man's Search for Himself

Introduction

This is a handbook of special experiences to
share with your children to help give them a
sense of identity and a feeling of self-worth.
It is hoped that these experiences will help
them feel comfortable with themselves and
to find meaning in themselves and in the
world around them.

How children see themselves determines the
fullness of their lives. Their views of self affect
every aspect of their lives—their emotions,
behavior, and ability to reach their individual
potential. It affects everything they do and can
become. Helping children form a "whole-some"
self-concept is one of our most important
challenges.

With this in mind, these activities were
designed to assist children in forming an early
positive vision as a base for their lifelong
interaction with the world. To give them a frame
of reference from which they can respond more
fully to life, this book includes experiences that
will help children to:

- Find a sense of rootedness in themselves and
  a sense of belonging to their own family,
  their extended family, and the entire human
  family.

- Accept their own bodies, thoughts, and
  feelings and feel accepted by others.

- Show care and responsibility for others and feel care from others.

- Be both independent and interdependent, happy with their individual selves, and willing to reach out to others.

- Realize inner, as well as outer, growth in an ever-changing world.

These experiences are generally intended for three-to nine-year-old children, but there are no hard-and-fast age guidelines. The activities can be adapted and enjoyed by children of various ages. They focus on children feeling comfortable with themselves alone, in the family, and in the world. However, these categories are not separated in this manner in the following pages, but are woven throughout the activities. Using these activities, you will be able to learn more about your "inner children" and thus be better able to understand and respond to their needs. You will also be able to stimulate their creativity, which, in turn, can add to their sense of achievement.

The experiences are designed so that parents may work with their children in an at-home situation or in a parent-child workshop setting. They are useful for anyone who works in early-childhood education. No matter how these activities are used, they can help children who are just beginning the lifelong process of finding joyful fulfillment in themselves by helping them grow in freedom and responsibility and in all that is truly human.

1. My Family Tree

How, then, can man tolerate this insecurity inherent in human existence? One way is to be rooted in the group in such a way that the feeling of identity is guaranteed by the membership to the group, be it family, clan, nation, class.

Erich Fromm,
The Sane Society

Figure A

PURPOSE
To help children:

- feel security in belonging.

- find a rootedness in themselves.

- learn more about their identity and realize that they are part of an extended family.

- understand that "making a family" is part of an ongoing process in which all members share.

- discover that family members have individual as well as common characteristics and that individuality can exist in unity.

SUGGESTED MATERIALS
For each family tree you will need:

- One sheet of poster board or card stock, at least 12 x 18 inches

- Marking pens with washable inks and/or water-soluble crayons or regular crayons

- Colored construction paper

- Double-stick tape or paste

- Pencil, scissors

Activity

1. Draw, or have children draw, an outline of a tree similar to the one in Figure A. Print names of parents on the trunk and children's names on the branches.

2. Make various "leaves" from the colored construction paper and mark these with

identifying traits, responsibilities or activities of each family member.

3. Explain as you go along that this tree can help children show what their family is like. To do this they should attach the leaves to the representative branches with tape or paste, thus identifying each individual's characteristics.

4. This activity can be extended by printing the names of each set of grandparents on the trunks of sketches you have made of two other trees (Figure B). Print the names of uncles and aunts on the main branches of each family tree and the names of their children on the smaller branches. Make corresponding sets of leaves for each extended family member. Explain to your children that all of these people are part of their larger family. Talk about the characteristics of each family member as you help them place the leaves on each branch. Older children can print the family members' names on the branches and think of traits for the various family leaves.

Figure B

2. Jiggety-Jaggety Puzzle

This early sense of self is highly unstable and is easily threatened with extinction. It retains its continuity only by stimulation from without.

Joseph Church,
Understanding Your Child
From Birth to Three

PURPOSE

To help children:

- see that the complete family is made up of all members and that each member's contribution is important to the total picture.
- realize that furniture, books, food, and clothing are part of what makes a home.

SUGGESTED MATERIALS

For each puzzle you will need:

- One sheet of poster board or card stock, approximately 12 x 18 inches
- Marking pens with washable inks and/or water-soluble crayons or regular crayons
- Photographs of family members, drawings of family members, or representative pictures of family members cut from old magazines
- Heavy object to weigh down pasted puzzle
- Pencil, paste, scissors
- Optional: old magazines

Activity

1. Label the photos, drawings, or pictures with the names of family members and paste them on the poster board. Weight this to hold it until dry. Then mark the resulting picture with irregular jigsaw puzzle lines. Cut the puzzle apart on the lines, mix up the pieces, and place them on a table.

2. Explain to your children that these are pieces of your family and that together they make a complete family. Help them put the puzzle together to make a family. You might say such things as: "See what happens when I take away your picture? The family picture is no longer complete."

3. The activity can be varied by using the pictures of members of your extended family or by including inanimate objects that make up a home: furniture, books, food, clothing, and so on.

4. Each puzzle can be kept in a manila envelope and labeled accordingly. Children may decorate each envelope as they wish.

3. A Poster-Picture of "Me"

Every person's primary life-relationship is to himself. The first creative venture he undertakes—long before he realizes its significance—is the building of the self-image.

Bonaro Overstreet,
*Understanding Fear
in Ourselves and in Others*

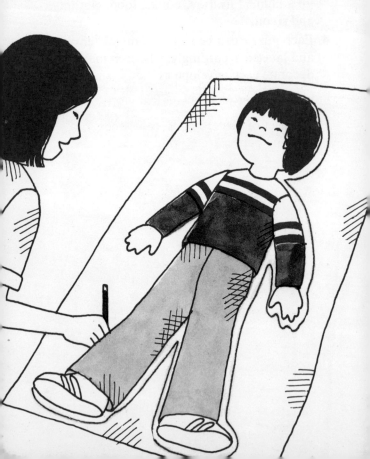

PURPOSE

To help children:

- visualize themselves in ways other than looking in a mirror.

- like, accept, and be at home with their own bodies.

- feel comfortable with, and learn more about, themselves.

- become aware of their emotions, thoughts, and wishes and feel free to express them.

- consider how they like to be treated and how they should treat others.

SUGGESTED MATERIALS

For each poster-picture you will need:

- One sheet of poster board, card stock, or wrapping paper large enough for a full-sized outline of a child

- Marking pens with washable inks and/or water-soluble crayons or regular crayons

- Old magazines or catalogs

- Double-stick tape or paste

- Picture hanger, cord, paper punch

- Pencil, scissors

- Optional: string, buttons, fabric, labeling cards

Activity

1. Lay the poster board or paper on the floor and

have your child lie on it. Trace around him or her to make an individual, silhouetted outline.

2. Cut out, or have your child cut out, the resulting poster-picture. If paper is used for the outline, it can be pasted on the poster-board backing. Identify the picture with your child's name.

3. You could say such things as: "This is a poster-picture of you. You can make it more like yourself by coloring it with the pens or crayons, taping things to it (string, buttons, fabric), or drawing on it in any way you wish. You may even cut out pictures from magazines or catalogs that tell something about yourself and paste them on your picture. You might want to cut out pictures of things you like to eat, friends you would like to have, and toys you would like to play with. And you might like to cut out pictures of children who show feelings that you, too, sometimes have—feelings such as happiness, sadness, or fear."

4. The pictures showing feelings could be placed in a box and added to the picture-posters at a later time. This could be an ongoing activity, with each child adding or changing feelings depending on his or her moods. This will help children see that life is a process of change and that change is a part of the process of growth.

5. Discussions might be held on the subjects of rights, responsibilities, ways of being treated, and ways of treating others. Children's

comments should be printed on their own poster-pictures or on small labels that can be attached to the poster-pictures.

6. To facilitate the changing of pictures and comments, punch a hole at the top of each poster-picture, attach a cord loop, and hang it on the wall. Urge children to change or add to the poster-picture as they wish.

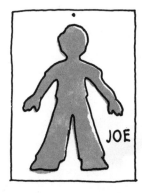

4. My Feeling Clock

Accepting negative feelings provides emotional relief, avoids repression, and teaches a child that he is no less worthy because of his feelings. He can remain in touch with himself as he truly is and be accepting of the humanness of others. . . . Releasing feelings helps youngsters see their problems more realistically rather than through the haze of heated emotion.

Dorothy Corkille Briggs,
Your Child's Self-Esteem

PURPOSE
To help children:

- realize that having feelings, even negative ones, is OK.

- express, not repress, their feelings in nonverbal as well as verbal ways.

- understand that they are accepted even when they express their feelings.

- grow in internal as well as external ways.

SUGGESTED MATERIALS
For each clock you will need:

- One sheet of poster board or card stock, approximately 12 x 18 inches, or one large paper plate

- One sheet of colored construction paper, approximately 8½ x 11 inches

- Marking pens with washable inks and/or water-soluble crayons or regular crayons

- One-inch metal paper fastener, paper punch

- Artist's compass

- Pencil, scissors

Activity

1. With an artist's compass, draw a large circle on the poster board or use a paper plate for a clock face. At regularly spaced intervals on the circumference of the circle, print various feelings: angry, sad, tired, disappointed,

afraid, loving, embarrassed, and so on. You might say to your children: "This is a feeling clock we are making. When it is finished, it will show just what feelings we have." Ask your children: "What feelings would you like to have me print on your clock face?" An older child can print his or her own feelings.

2. Using the colored paper, make two 1-inch by 4-inch arrows for each member of the family. Arrows might also be made for relatives and friends. Print family or friends' names on the arrows.

3. Punch holes in the center of the clock and also about ½ inch from the blunt end of each arrow. Attach these arrows to the clock with the metal paper fastener.

4. Explain that members of the family can show what feelings they have by moving their arrows to the corresponding feeling on each child's clock. Children can show their feelings about other family members by placing their arrow over the arrow of the person they are happy or unhappy with or have a feeling about.

5. A Calendar of Me

Most contemporary psychotherapy, as typified in the current enthusiasm for Transactional Analysis and its central goal of learning to feel Okay, is designed to help a person towards one thing: to help him adopt a kindly, positive and accepting attitude towards himself. Most people are very far from this, even though we could easily be deceived by surface attitudes.

John Powell,
The Secret of Staying in Love

PURPOSE

To help children:

- learn that liking oneself is OK.

- learn that being unhappy with oneself is OK.

- understand that being unhappy with oneself does not mean disliking oneself.

- realize that people do not have to be perfect in order to accept themselves or to be accepted by others.

SUGGESTED MATERIALS

For each calendar you will need:

- One sheet of poster board or card stock, approximately 12 x 18 inches

- Marking pens with washable inks and/or water-soluble crayons or regular crayons

- Picture hanger, cord, paper punch

- Pencil, ruler

Activity

1. Mark off a 3-inch margin from the 18-inch length of the poster board. Then mark off the remaining 12 x 15 inches into appropriate sections for each day of the month, leaving room at the top for abbreviations of days of the week.

2. In the margin of the calendar, list adjectives or nouns appropriate to members of your family: patient, kind, good cook, artist, teacher, mother, father, wage earner or the like.

3. Explain to your children that there are things we *like* and *dislike* about ourselves, but that for the first week you will fill in the blank spaces with something you *like* about yourself. For the first week they may also fill in (or ask you to fill in) something they *like* about themselves.

4. Tell your children that for the second week you will fill in the blank spaces with something you are *happy* with; they may do the same. Explain that if they do not wish to write anything about themselves, they may draw something about themselves.

5. Tell children that for the last two weeks of the month, you will fill in anything you wish about yourself—either something that you are happy with or something you are unhappy with, and that they may do the same. Talk to them in everyday conversation of this. You can say things such as: "I am angry with myself for getting a parking ticket. I am sorry that I left the water running." Help your children see that it is alright to feel unhappy as well as happy with themselves.

6. Keep your calendar filled in as much as possible, but do not demand that your children maintain a daily interest. Hanging your calendar in a prominent spot and filling it in as faithfully as possible will do much to keep up your children's interest level in their calendars.

6. A Person We Love

If we cannot love ourselves, where will we draw our love for anyone else?
Mildred Newman and Bernard Berkowitz,
How to Be Your Own Best Friend

PURPOSE
To help children:

- express how they feel about themselves and get to know themselves better.
- pinpoint the people they are involved with.
- find acceptance despite what they say or what their feelings are.
- become comfortable in expressing what they like about themselves.
- find a sense of importance in seeing their words "in print."

SUGGESTED MATERIALS
For each story you will need:

- Writing paper
- Marking pens with washable inks and/or water-soluble crayons or regular crayons
- Pencil, ruler

Activity

Print the following story or an adaptation of it for each child, ruling in blanks as shown. Then read the story to your children. Explain that it is about a person you all love (oneself) and that the story is not a story unless each child tells you what to write or draw. Modify the story according to your own family situation. An older child will be able to complete the story without aid.

This is my story.

My name is _____.

I live at _____.

My telephone number is _____.

I have a daddy named _____.

My daddy is _____.

I have a mother named _____.

My mother is _____.

I have a _____ (brother, sister, friend, aunt, uncle, grandma, grandpa).

My brother's name is _____.

My sister's name is _____.

My grandma's name is _____.

My grandpa's name is _____.

My other grandma's name is _____.

My other grandpa's name is _____.

I have an aunt whose name is _____, and an aunt named _____.

Sometimes I play with my friends. Their names are _____ and _____.

I like to play _____.

I like _____.

I am happy when _____.

I am sad when _____.

I am sorry when _____.

I am afraid when _____.

I am angry when _____.

I am embarrassed when _____.

These are the people who love me: _____,

_____,

_____.

They love me because _____.

I like me because _____.

7. Family Puppetry

*I am capable of accepting . . . of enjoying and
celebrating the differences in human beings.*
Bob Samples and Bob Wohlford,
Opening

PURPOSE
To help children:

- see likeness and differences in others.

- reconstruct family activities out of their own imaginations.

- role-play various members of the family and express how they see and what they feel about the various roles.

- understand that individuality and unity are part of belonging to a family.

- learn to be more at home with themselves as they think about and role-play different individuals.

SUGGESTED MATERIALS
For puppets representing all family members you will need a quantity of:

- Poster board or card stock
- Construction paper
- Various lengths of flat balsa wood sticks
- Marking pens with washable inks and/or water-soluble crayons or regular crayons
- Old soft socks
- Scissors, paste
- Needles, thread, buttons, small safety pins, fabric, paper sacks

Activity

1. Let your children help you design puppets

to represent each member of your family. Use these suggestions:

Make puppets out of paper sacks and let children decorate them as they choose. Cut holes in the sides for finger arms and show children how to use marking pens to paint on face, body, and clothing. Place your or your child's hand inside sack to manipulate.

Show children how to sew scraps of fabric or buttons on to soft socks to represent puppets with eyes, ears, nose, mouth, clothing, and so on. Place on your or your child's hand to manipulate.

Help children paste construction paper to a flat stick to fashion a head and clothing. Fabric may be pasted on the construction-paper clothing.

2. Print the name of each family member on the appropriate puppet.

3. Suggest to children that they act out various family situations with their puppets, make up a play about their family, or play "Let's pretend."

8. Floor Plans

The home is, for better or worse, the place where the child meets not only those all-important persons who are his parents but also diverse samples of the human race. It is therefore the place where he begins to enjoy those others or to fear them; to share with them, or to hold his own against them, or to grab from them; treat them as equals, or as superiors or inferiors.

Bonaro Overstreet,
*Understanding Fear in
Ourselves and in Others*

PURPOSE

To help children:

- feel a sense of identity with their home.

- express how they feel about their homes and/or rooms.

- learn how to share feelings.

SUGGESTED MATERIALS

For each floor plan you will need:

- Two sheets of poster board or card stock, approximately 8½ x 11 inches

- Marking pens with washable inks and/or water-soluble crayons or regular crayons

- Pencil, ruler

Activity

1. Draw a floor plan of one floor of your home.

2. Have your children draw a floor plan of their home, using yours as a pattern.

3. Explain to your children that you are going to color your favorite room with a specially selected color. Decorate the floor plan in any way you wish; then have your children color their favorite room and decorate it any way they wish. Have them tell you about their drawings.

4. As an alternate activity, you might make a floor plan of just your favorite room, drawing in furniture and other items. Children may do the same, decorating their favorite room as they wish.

9. The People We Are

In all the world, there is no one else exactly like me. There are persons who have some parts like me but no one adds up exactly like me.

Virginia Satir,
Making Contact

PURPOSE

To help children:

• learn to categorize.

• focus on a person's individuality and perceive that groups are made up of individuals.

• see that both likenesses and differences can be observed in a family.

• learn how to view themselves and other family members.

SUGGESTED MATERIALS

For each set of cards you will need:

• One sheet of lightweight poster board or card stock, approximately 4 x 15 inches, or five old playing cards

• Marking pens with washable inks and/or water-soluble crayons or regular crayons

• Photographs of family members or magazine pictures representing them

• Pencil, ruler, paste, scissors

• Optional: old magazines

Activity

1. Cut a set of five cards, approximately 3 x 4 inches, for each member of the family.
   Five old playing cards may also be used.

2. Paste a photo, drawing, or magazine picture representing each member of the family on one card in each set. Identify this card with the name of the family member.

3. On the remaining cards in each set, print or paste pictures of some activity, characteristic, or identifying quality of each family member. For example, individual cards could be labeled or illustrated with words such as: has toy box, owns a dog, drives a car, is 3 years old, wears a man's suit, carries a purse, works in the garden, plants flowers, reads books, is in first grade. Be sure that each set has the same number of identifying cards.
4. Explain to your children that the object of this game is to match a family member's name and face with the characteristics of that person. Include cards that describe feelings and cards that could fit several members of the family. Be sure, however, that each card fits at least one family member.
5. Place all the cards, picture-side down, on the table. Players alternate in drawing the cards. No card is to be laid face up until a player has drawn a "person" card. When a "person" card is drawn and placed on the table, that player can match whatever other card is in his or her hand to the corresponding "person." According to turn, any player may match any appropriate card to the corresponding "person" card on the table. When all the cards are drawn from the center of the table, the player with the most cards matched to a person wins. (If you use only labels on the cards, you might have to read these to the children, but they should judge what person fits with the label.)

10. My Kinship Wall

A series of facts unites mankind—all mankind.
Gordon Allport,
Existential Psychology

PURPOSE

To help children:

- learn who comprise their extended family and begin to establish a bond with them.

- see that extended family members are important to them.

- become closer to relatives whom they do not know, whom they seldom see, or who are deceased.

- gain a feeling of security and identity through knowledge of their forebears.

SUGGESTED MATERIALS

For the kinship wall you will need:

- Photographs or sketches of relatives, including grandparents, aunts, uncles, cousins

- Inexpensive frames

- Optional: pegboard with hooks; heavy poster board; paste, glue, or double-stick tape

Activity

1. Place photographs in inexpensive frames and make a wall grouping which can become part of your home, or hang framed photographs on pegboard which can be moved from place to place or hung on the wall. If frames are not available, attach photographs or sketches of extended family members to a large sheet of heavy poster board with paste, glue, or double-stick tape.

2. Talk to your children about members of their extended family. Tell about the things they did, what they were like, and what they are like now. Help your children see that these family members are or were real people.

11. Fairy Tales and Feelings

The fairy-tale hero proceeds for a time in isolation, as the modern child often feels isolated. The hero is helped by being in touch with primitive things—a tree, an animal, nature—as the child feels more in touch with those things than most adults do. The fate of these heroes convinces the child that, like them, he may feel outcast and abandoned in the world, groping in the dark, but, like them, in the course of his life he will be guided step by step, and given help when it is needed. Today, even more than in past times, the child needs the reassurance offered by the image of the isolated man who nevertheless is capable of achieving meaningful and rewarding relations with the world around him.

Bruno Bettelheim,
*The Uses of Enchantment:
The Meaning and Importance of Fairy Tales*

PURPOSE

To help children:

• learn something about coping with life by listening to fairy tales.

• appreciate a work of literature and draw inner resources from it.

• imagine themselves in various roles.

• be able to express their feelings about a story in verbal and nonverbal ways.

SUGGESTED MATERIALS

You will need:

• Assorted books of fairy tales suited to your children's ages

• Butcher paper, index cards, or lightweight card stock

• Marking pens with washable inks and/or water-soluble crayons or regular crayons

• Finger paints, or liquid starch and food coloring, in small containers

• Optional: pieces of sponge and spring clothespins to be used as paintbrushes

Activity

1. Make a practice of reading fairy tales to your children. When you finish a story, talk with your children about it. Ask them how they would feel if they were some character in the story. If you have just read *Cinderella,* for example, ask the children how they would feel

if they were the wicked stepmother, one of the stepsisters, the prince charming, or the fairy godmother.

2. Give children finger paints (or liquid starch and food coloring), butcher paper (or index cards or lightweight card stock), and marking pens (or crayons or "brushes"). Let them paint what the story was about, then tell you about their drawings.

12. The "All About Me" Book

Every person born in this world represents something new, something that never existed before, something original and unique.
Martin Buber
To Hallow This Life

PURPOSE

To help children:

- focus on their own individuality and also on their similarity to others.

- realize that individual preferences may vary and that these variations are acceptable.

- recognize different aspects or characteristics of themselves.

SUGGESTED MATERIALS

For each book you will need:

- Sheets of wrapping paper, butcher paper or typing paper

- Two sheets of construction paper, 9 x 12 inches

- Marking pens with washable inks and/or water-soluble crayons or regular crayons

- Old magazines or catalogs

- Cord to lace book together, paper punch

- Pencil, paste, scissors

Activity

1. Assist each child in cutting twenty-eight 9 x 12-inch pieces of wrapping paper, butcher paper, or the like. Punch holes in each sheet, 4 inches from the top and 1 inch from the side of each edge. Do the same with the two sheets of construction paper. Place one sheet on top of the twenty-eight sheets and one on the bottom as covers. Tie together with cord to form a book.

2. Label, or have your child label, the book: All About Me.

3. Label, or have your child label, every four pages with the following suggested titles or with any others that would be appropriate:
   Things I Like to Do
   Places I Like to Visit
   Food I Like to Eat
   Clothes I Like to Wear
   Friends Like Mine
   In My House I Would Like to Have . . .
   Pets I Would Like to Take Care of . . .
   Work I Would Like to Do

4. Explain to your children that these are their own books in which they will be able to tell all about themselves. They may cut pictures from magazines or catalogs and paste them in the appropriate sections. They may also draw pictures or write lists if they are old enough. If possible, have your children print their own names or initials on their title pages and design covers for their own books.

13. We Help Build the World

By his fidelity he must build—starting with the most natural territory of his own self—a work, an opus, into which something enters from all the elements of the earth . . . and at the same time he collaborates in another work . . . the completing of the world.

Pierre Teilhard de Chardin,
The Divine Milieu

MY WORLD

AT HOME

AT SCHOOL

AT GYM CLASS

WITH FRIENDS

AT GRANDMA'S HOUSE

PURPOSE

To help children:

- see that they belong to a wider world than just the family and that their actions are important in building it.

- understand that the world is shaped by the actions of individuals.

- recognize the importance of their own contributions to building the world in everyday living.

SUGGESTED MATERIALS

For each "world" you will need:

- One sheet of poster board, approximately 12 x 18 inches

- Marking pens with washable inks and/or water-soluble crayons or regular crayons

- Small pieces of colored paper

- Double-stick tape

- Artist's compass

Activity

1. With an artist's compass, draw a circle on the poster board. Mark it into irregularly shaped sections, as shown in the illustration.

2. Ask your children to imagine that this is the *world* you are drawing, and that each of the sections represents one part of their action in the world. Label these sections according

to children's level of participation in home and outside activities, such as:

At School
With My Friends
At Home
At Gym Class
My Home Jobs

3. Tell children that they are to write or draw within each section anything that shows what they do in each of those areas of their life. (You might help children get started on this activity by showing how *you* yourself would fill in a world with *your* activities.) If they wish, children can draw, print, or have you print separate activities for each section on small pieces of colored paper. These could be attached to the different areas which make up their world.

4. Explain that the world is made up of the individual activities of every single person, and that children help "build the world" with everything they do.

14. When I'm Alone, When I'm with Others

Solitude is nearly a misnomer. To me, being alone means togetherness—the re-coming together of me and nature, of me and being; the reuniting of me with all. For me, solitude especially means putting the parts of me back together—the unifying of myself whereby I see once again that the little things are little and the big things are big.

I believe that solitude is a profound and needed act of self-love and self-appreciation.

Hugh Prather,
Notes to Myself

WHEN I'M ALONE
I LIKE TO

WHEN I'M WITH OTHERS
I LIKE TO

SAM

SAM

PURPOSE

To help children:

- learn to enjoy activities alone as well as with others.

- realize that being alone and being with others is part of being themselves.

- see that preferences can change or be added to as a part of growth.

SUGGESTED MATERIALS

For each child you will need:

- One sheet of poster board or card stock, 18 x 24 inches

- Marking pens with washable inks and/or water-soluble crayons or regular crayons

- Old magazines or catalogs

- Double-stick tape, paper punch

- Picture hanger, cord

- Pencil, ruler, scissors

- Optional: ten or more sheets of paper 8½ x 11 inches and three sheets of construction paper

Activity

1. Mark off a 6-inch margin at the top of the 24-inch length of the poster board, leaving an 18 x 18-inch section.

2. Divide this section lengthwise into two 9 x 18-inch sections.

3. Write these two titles in the sections:

When I'm Alone, I Like to . . . When I'm with Others, I Like to . . .

4. Draw a circle representing a child's head in each top portion of the poster board and sketch a stick figure in the remaining section. Label both stick figures with your child's name.

5. Explain that these two drawings represent the person we are when are alone and the person we are when we are with others.

6. Suggest that children cut pictures from magazines or catalogs that show things they like to do by themselves and things they like to do with others. They may also draw suitable pictures in each column or tell you appropriate words to write about their preferences. Older children will be able to write their own words.

7. The two-person drawing can be punched at the top, looped with cord, and hung on the wall, to be added to whenever your child wishes.

8. As an alternate activity, make a book using sheets of 8½ x 11-inch paper with colored construction paper for the covers and a middle divider of the book. Punch holes and lace together. Identify each section according to the above titles. Children may then fill the book with pictures, drawings, or words illustrating what they like to do alone and with others.

15. A Home Is Where We Care and Share

In the very act of assessing the human condition and developing the patterns for prescription, two generations of psychologists denied in their evaluations the fundamental characteristics of human beings . . . compassion . . . communication . . . commitment.

Bob Samples and Bob Wohlford,
Opening

A HOME IS WHERE WE CARE... WHERE WE SHARE									
	TASKS	S	M	T	W	T	F	S	FOR THE WEEK
CHRIS									
LIZ									
LEAH									
STACY									
JILL									

54

PURPOSE
To help children:

- realize a sense of accomplishment through taking on responsibilities.

- understand that sharing responsibilities indicates love and caring, which are important in a family.

- create a visible record of their accomplishments for themselves and others to observe.

- learn how to evaluate their successes and failures and how to accept evaluation from others.

SUGGESTED MATERIALS
For each chart you will need:

- One sheet of poster board or card stock large enough to accomodate a chart of various activities of all family members

- Marking pens with washable inks and/or water-soluble crayons or regular crayons

- Small pieces of construction paper or card stock to make into labeling circles

- Double-stick tape, paper punch

- Picture hanger, cord

- Pencil, ruler

Activity

1. Make a family sharing chart similar to the one illustrated. Leave a margin of 2 inches on the left side of the chart and print in the names

of all family members. Next to the names, mark off a 2-inch column in which various responsibilities of each family member may be listed.

2. As you are doing this, ask your children to think about the responsibilities they would like to share in helping the family be a family. Suggest responsibilities you think they can handle. Mark off the remaining portion of the chart as indicated, leaving a space at the right of the chart in which children may evaluate their own week.

3. Children should now print, or tell you to print, what tasks or responsibilities they will share each day of the week. They may decorate their charts with their own artwork if they wish.

4. Make three 1-inch circles for each family member. One circle should show a happy face or the word "OK"; one should show a sad face or the words "Not OK"; the third should be left blank.

5. Explain that at the end of each day, each family member will show how he or she felt about doing the task or tasks assigned by attaching the appropriate labeling circle to that day. If the feeling was OK, for instance, the happy face should be attached; if the responsibility was not fulfilled, the blank circle should be attached. Move the circles at the end of each day, but keep track of which circle was attached with penciled notation.

6. By the end of the week, children should be able to evaluate themselves as to how well they have helped the family and fulfilled their responsibilities. They may then attach one of the three labeling circles according to how they judged their work and their week. Explain that you will also evaluate their work; if you agree with their evaluation, you will put your initials above their evaluation.

16. My House, Our House

> *Love and self-worth are so intertwined that they may properly be related through the use of the term* identity. *Thus we may say that the single basic need that people have is the requirement for an identity: the belief that we are someone is distinction to others, and that the someone is important and worthwhile. Then* love and self-worth may be considered the two pathways that mankind has discovered lead to a successful identity.

William Glasser,
Schools Without Failure

PURPOSE

To help children:

- focus on themselves and see that their activities make up a "House of Myself."

- realize that the combining of activities makes a home.

- recognize the individuality and interdependence of all human beings.

- develop a sense of their own worth and the worth of others.

SUGGESTED MATERIALS

For each child you will need:

- Three or more sheets of poster board or card stock, 9 x 12 inches

- Colored construction paper

- Marking pens with washable inks and/or water-soluble crayons or regular crayons

- Double-stick tape or paste

- Pencil, scissors

Activity

1. Draw an outline of a house on each of three or more sheets of poster board. (You will need three for yourself and one child, and one more for each additional child.) Make one of the houses larger than the others. Label them as shown in the illustration. Cut out at least one dozen small rectangular pieces of construction paper "bricks" for each house.

2. Explain to your children that each of them can build a "House of Myself" by telling you to write on their bricks whatever they do in their house. They can then "build" their houses by pasting or taping on the bricks. Activities children mention might include:
   sleeping
   playing with dog
   taking care of kitten
   cooking eggs for breakfast
   watching TV
   Older children, of course, can label their own bricks.
3. Explain that you will also participate by printing activities you engage in in your house on separate brick pieces of paper. Attach your bricks to the smaller house picture you have reserved for yourself.
4. Label the small houses: House of Myself.
5. Now, remove all bricks from these houses, and alternate in placing the individual bricks on the large house. Label this house: Our Home. Point out that it is the activities of all family members combined that makes a home.

17. I Help the Sun Shine

Through caring for certain others, by serving them through caring, a man lives the meaning of his own life. In the sense in which a man can ever be said to be at home in the world, he is at home not through dominating, or explaining, or appreciating, but through caring and being cared for.

To care for another person, in the most significant sense, is to help him grow and actualize himself.

Milton Mayeroff,
On Caring

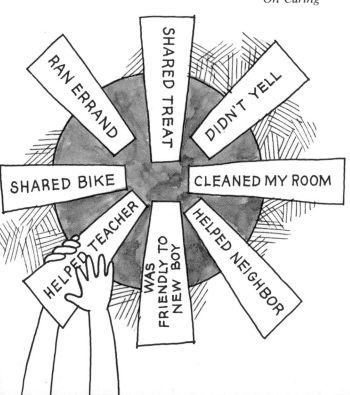

PURPOSE

To help children:

- realize that they can help others grow by caring and showing that they care.

- focus on how they are cared for by others.

- understand that caring for and being kind to others can contribute to their own happiness.

SUGGESTED MATERIALS

For each sun you will need:

- One sheet of poster board or card stock, approximately 12 x 12 inches

- Several sheets of yellow construction paper, at least one of which is 16 x 20 inches

- Marking pens with washable inks and/or water-soluble crayons or regular crayons

- Double-stick tape or paste

- Artist's compass

- Pencil, scissors

Activity

1. With an artist's compass, draw a 12-inch circle on the construction paper. Cut out this circle and also eight tapered rectangular 2 x 5-inch pieces of yellow paper.

2. Explain to your children that the yellow circle represents the sun and the tapered pieces of yellow paper represent the rays from the sun shining on people around them.

3. Have children paste the sun on the sheet of poster board and tell them that they can help the sun shine by making the world brighter for others with such things as smiles, hellos, acts of kindness and politeness, and so on. Ask them to suggest kind and polite actions that might be printed on each ray. Label each sun chart with a child's name.

4. Tell children that each time they help the sun shine on someone around them, they may place the proper descriptive ray on their sun, using double-stick tape or paste.

5. As a variation, follow the same procedure as above, but let children add rays to their suns whenever they have received a kindness or polite action from another.

18. This Is the Way We Build Our Home

Even as he separates himself from that to which he responds, he remains related at the same time. In the very act of becoming aware of his individuality, the capacity for relatedness develops. Isolation and alienation are terrifying experiences; in relatedness there is peace.

Antonia Wenkart,
"The Child Meets the World"
Existential Child Therapy:
The Child's Discovery of Himself

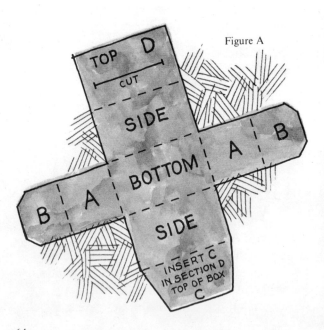

Figure A

PURPOSE

To help children:

- learn that a family is composed of individuals with varying dispositions, characteristics, and responsibilities.

- recognize the importance of each family member.

- feel more at home with themselves as they accept similarities and differences in others.

- realize that they have a vital role in building a home.

SUGGESTED MATERIALS

For each family member you will need:

- Four pieces of poster board or card stock, 8 x 8 inches square

- Marking pens with washable inks and/or water-soluble crayons or regular crayons

- Scratch paper

- Cellophane tape

- Pencil, ruler, scissors

Activity

1. Cut poster board according to the pattern in Figure A. Fold into boxes. Make four boxes for each family member, and label them with the appropriate names. Have children help you make a list of strengths, activities, contributions, responsibilities, work, hobbies,

likes, and dislikes of the various family members and print these on the boxes for each person. Boxes may also be decorated with drawings representing individual family activities.

2. Explain to your children that everything that is part of a member of the family is part of the whole family. Then show how the boxes of each one's characteristics can be stacked, one upon the other, and arranged to build a house (see Figure B).

3. Read labels on the boxes to your children if they cannot read. Choose one of your boxes first. Then have one of your children choose another box and add it to your box. Continue "building" the house together as you read to your children the family characteristics and activities that go into building a home.

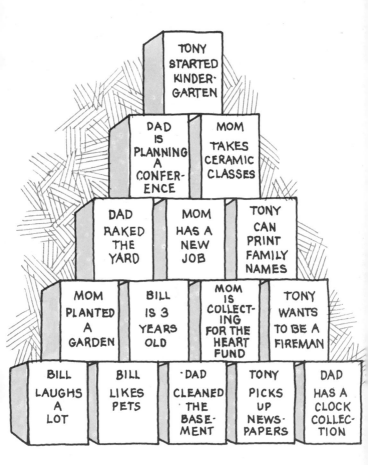

Figure B

19. My World and Me

I will never be able to find myself if I isolate myself from the rest of mankind as if I were a different kind of being.

Thomas Merton,
Seeds of Contemplation

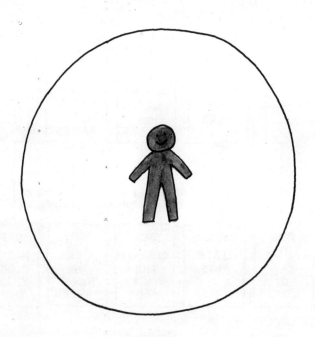

Figure A

PURPOSE

To help children:

- realize that they are a vital part of the world, as are their family and friends.

- see that homes, places of business, and institutions help make up the world.

- see how each of them fits into this picture of the world as he or she knows it at a particular age.

- value the people and institutions found in their world.

SUGGESTED MATERIALS

For each child you will need:

- One sheet of poster board or card stock, approximately 18 x 24 inches

- Several sheets of lightweight card stock or construction paper

- Marking pens with washable inks and/or water-soluble crayons or regular crayons

- Double-stick tape

- Pencil, scissors

- Optional: old magazines or catalogs

- Artist's compass

Activity

1. Draw, or have your child draw, one large circle on the poster board to represent the world.

2. Using the card stock or construction paper, draw one figure similar to the example in the center of Figure A. Cut the figure out and print the child's name on it. Attach it with double-stick tape to the center of "the world."

3. Draw and cut out a variety of figures of different sizes representing other family members. Print names on all figures and have children place those around the central figure of the child, attaching them with double-stick tape.

4. If desired, draw and cut out additional figures to represent friends, relatives, and acquaintances. Print names on these figures and let children attach them around the family figures.

5. Draw or cut from magazines or catalogs pictures of buildings, trees, and landmarks to represent the child's own home and other homes and buildings with which he is familiar: homes of friends or relatives, stores, schools, churches, and so on. Children should suggest what items might be included. Arrange these in "the world" as shown in Figure B.

6. While you are carrying out this activity, explain that our world is made of ourselves, our family, our friends, the homes of friends, the buildings in which people work or assemble, and the world of nature.

Figure B

20. How Many Ways Have I Grown?

The child, being himself, is continually enhanced by becoming himself.

Antonia Wenkart,
"The Child Meets the World"
Existential Child Therapy:
The Child's Discovery of Himself

A growing person is self-renewing . . . as new as each day. . . . Study his face and hands, listen to his voice . . . look for change. . . . It is certain that he has changed.

John Powell,
Why Am I Afraid
to Tell You Who I Am?

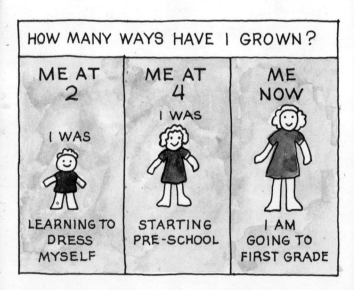

HOW MANY WAYS HAVE I GROWN?

ME AT 2	ME AT 4	ME NOW
I WAS	I WAS	
LEARNING TO DRESS MYSELF	STARTING PRE-SCHOOL	I AM GOING TO FIRST GRADE

PURPOSE

To help children:

- see that change is a normal part of life and that we need not fear it.

- focus on inner growth as well as outer, physical growth.

- relish the idea of change and growth.

SUGGESTED MATERIALS

For yourself and each child you will need:

- One sheet of poster board or card stock, at least 12 x 18 inches

- Marking pens with washable inks and/or water-soluble crayons or regular crayons

- Pencil, scissors

Activity

1. Make a three-column chart similar to the one illustrated. Label it: The Many Ways I Have Grown.

2. In each column, draw a picture showing how *you* looked as a child, as an adult, and as you think you will look twenty years from now. Talk about the changes—how you changed in size and in other ways.

3. Make three-column charts for your children and ask them to draw how they looked at various ages in their life. For instance, a six-year-old girl could draw how she thinks she

looked as a two-year-old, as a four-year-old, and now.

4. Talk with children about the differences in their drawings and how they have grown in ways other than size; for example, how they can now walk to school by themselves, keep a record of their allowance, and so on. Observe how it feels to grow inside as well as outside—how an individual can become a new person while remaining essentially the same.

21. Pieces of Myself

"I've decided, Mom, I could be mad at you, and still love you and like you, too."

A three-year-old to his mother

PURPOSE

To help children:

- see that people embrace a wide range of characteristics, roles, and emotions and that all combine to make a whole person.

- understand that characteristics, roles, and emotions vary among people and even within an individual.

SUGGESTED MATERIALS

For yourself and each child you will need:

- One sheet of poster board or card stock, approximately 14 x 22 inches

- Several sheets of lightweight paper

- Marking pens with washable inks and/or water-soluble crayons or regular crayons

- Double-stick tape or paste

- Pencil

Activity

1. Make a large drawing of yourself on the poster board. On irregularly shaped pieces of paper, print your various qualities, roles, and emotions. Explain to your children that you are sometimes sad, happy, or afraid; that you are many different people: parent, spouse, cook, teacher, artist, student, wage earner, and so on. Paste or tape these various pieces describing yourself on the outline of yourself.

2. Draw, or have your children draw, outlines of themselves. Let children describe their own characteristics, roles, and emotions; print these for them on slips of paper.

3. Have children attach the slips of paper to their own outlines. Point out that these slips tell what each child is like as an individual.

4. If children prefer, they may draw pictures of their characteristics, roles, and emotions and attach these to their own outlines.

22. What Does My Shadow See?

I have a little shadow that goes in and out with me,
And what can be the use of him is more than I can see.
He is very, very like me from the heels up to the head,
And I see him jump before me when I jump into my bed.

Robert Louis Stevenson
A Child's Garden of Verses

WHAT DOES MY SHADOW SEE?

WAS SENT TO MY ROOM

WENT TO THE PARK

PLAYING WITH FRIENDS

FED MY DOG

WAS ANGRY AT DAD

GOT A BIRTHDAY PRESENT

PURPOSE
To help children:

- express how they might see themselves in different situations.

- see themselves more clearly and learn to depict themselves in real-life situations.

- practice looking at themselves in an objective manner.

SUGGESTED MATERIALS
For each child you will need:

- One sheet of poster board or card stock, approximately 14 x 22 inches

- Pieces of colored paper for six 2 x 4-inch labels

- Marking pens with washable inks and/or water-soluble crayons or regular crayons

- Double-stick tape

- Pencil, scissors

Activity

1. On the poster board, draw six mirrors as shown in the illustration. Label the drawing: What Does My Shadow See?

2. Help children list six places they went to or activities they participated in during the past week.

3. Write each of these places or activities on 2 x 4-inch labels. Have children attach them with double-stick tape beneath the mirrors—

one label under each mirror. The labels might
include:
Fed My Dog
Went to the Dentist
Played with Friends
Went to Day-Care Center
Was Sent to My Room
Told Mom and Dad I Was Mad at Them

4. Read the Stevenson verse to your children and
talk about what your shadows might see
during an ordinary day. Suggest that children
imagine that they are their own shadows.
Ask them to draw in each of the mirrors what
their shadows saw. (You may have to read the
mirror labels aloud to the children before they
can illustrate their shadow selves.) Ask such
questions as: "How do you think your shadow
saw you in each mirror? Do you think your
shadow liked what it saw? Why or why not?
What do you think your shadow would say
about you? What would your shadow
say about what you thought and felt?"

23. At Home in the World

You will find children absorbed in conversation with animals, flowers, dolls, on a footing of intimacy and equality; you will find in the myths and fairy tales which enshrine primitive wisdom the same sharing of life between man and the rest of creation.

Gerald Vann,
The Heart of Man

ROLLING IN THE GRASS

WALKING IN THE RAIN

SNOW BLOWING IN MY FACE

CLIMBING A HILL

RUNNING IN WIND

SWIMMING IN LAKE

PURPOSE

To help children:

- focus on their close relationship with the world of nature and envision their physical sensations in the "space" of the world.

- learn to express feelings both orally and visually.

- learn more about life through physical experiences, and relate these at a later time to their reading activities.

SUGGESTED MATERIALS

For each child you will need:

- Six sheets of poster board or card stock, 9 x 12 inches, or one sheet of poster board, 24 x 36 inches, divided into six sections

- Marking pens with washable inks and/or water-soluble crayons or regular crayons

- Pencil, scissors

Activity

This is a variation of the preceding activity, but it focuses on children's contact with nature.

1. Label each sheet or section of poster board with an outdoor activity that children enjoy, such as the following:

    Rolling in the Grass
    Walking in the Rain
    Climbing a Hill
    Running in the Wind

Having Snow Blow on My Face
Paddling or Swimming in the Lake or
the Ocean

2. Ask children to imagine how their shadows
felt doing each activity. Suggest that they
draw or paint an appropriate picture of their
shadows in each section.

24. Let My Fears Fly Away

The first step in overcoming fear is to acknowledge it. Because preschoolers closely identify with parents, a sound way to reduce harmful consequences of children's fear is for parents to admit their own fears. A child who is afraid of the dark, of being alone, or of starting school should be assured by grownups that fear is a natural reaction and that to acknowledge fear does not make one a coward.

Robert Strom,
"Play and Family Development"
Readings in Educational Psychology:
Contemporary Perspectives

PURPOSE

To help children:

- realize that the first step in overcoming fear is recognizing it.

- see that talking about their fears helps more than hiding them.

- feel that you accept (rather than deride) them with their fears.

- understand that everyone fears something and that there is nothing wrong with having fears.

SUGGESTED MATERIALS

For yourself and each child you will need:

- One sheet of poster board or card stock, approximately 12 x 18 inches

- Several sheets of colored construction paper, approximately 3 x 4 inches

- Several sheets of white scratch paper

- One small empty box

- Marking pens with washable inks and/or water-soluble crayons or regular crayons

- Pencil, ruler, scissors

Activity

1. Print on each empty box: My Fears. See that each child has a box with his or her own name on it.

2. Write on the small slips of scratch paper the various things you are afraid of. Put these in your box.

3. Help your children write down their fears on slips of scratch paper, depositing them in their own boxes.

4. Draw leaves on the colored construction paper and cut them out. Label each leaf with one of your own fears and place them, too, in your box.

5. Now have your children draw and cut out leaves, then label each with one of their fears. Let them put these into their own "fear" boxes.

6. Using the poster board, prepare for each child a neighborhood scene showing a broad expanse of sky as in the illustration. Label it: Let My Fears Fly Away.

7. Alternate with your children in drawing slips of scratch paper from the boxes. Talk about your fears and theirs. As soon as a fear has been talked about, you or a child may draw from the "fear" box the leaf that represents the corresponding fear.

8. Tape or paste the "fear leaf" to the sky in your neighborhood scene. Explain that this is how you will let your fears blow away.

9. As your children talk about each of their fears, they may also put the corresponding "fear leaf" in the sky of their picture where it, too, might blow away.

25. I Help the Candles Glow

Man can become whole not in virtue of a relation to himself but only in virtue of a relation to another self.

Martin Buber,
To Hallow This Life

PURPOSE

To help children:

- realize that friends help one another learn, grow, and be happy.

- see that friendship is a two-way street: that we must give happiness to friends as well as receive happiness from them.

- recognize that friends come in all sizes, sexes, ages, and backgrounds.

SUGGESTED MATERIALS

For each child you will need:

- One sheet of poster board or card stock, approximately 12 x 18 inches

- Yellow construction paper, approximately 4 x 6 inches

- Other colored construction paper, at least 9 x 12 inches

- Double-stick tape or paste

- Pencil, ruler, scissors

Activity

1. Talk to your children about friendship—how friends help us grow and how they help light us up with happiness. As friends help us feel good about ourselves, so we can help them feel good about themselves. Explain that this activity can help us visualize and think about the people who are our friends.

2. Help children draw candles on the 9 x 12-inch construction paper to represent their friends. Sizes may vary to indicate children and adults. Label each candle with the friend's name.

3. Tape or paste the candles in a row on the poster board. Cut flames from the yellow construction paper and attach above each candle. Label the chart: These Are My Friends.

4. Remind children again that friends help light up our lives. They are like candles glowing in the darkness. Urge children to talk about how they help light up their friend's lives.

26. Star Light, Star Bright

Star light, star bright/
First star I see tonight.
I wish I may, I wish I might/
Have the wish I wish tonight.

Nursery Rhyme

PURPOSE
To help children:

- see that they have some control over attaining their own goals and making their own wishes come true.

- sort out wishes that are realistic from those that are unlikely to come true.

- feel good about helping themselves attain a goal.

SUGGESTED MATERIALS
For each child you will need:

- One sheet of poster board or card stock, approximately 12 x 18 inches

- Several sheets of yellow construction paper

- Double-stick tape

- Pencil, ruler, scissors

Activity

1. Write the nursery rhyme at the top of the length of poster board for each child, as shown on the illustration.
2. Help children draw and cut out stars from the yellow construction paper to represent their wishes. Label them and attach them with double-stick tape directly beneath the rhyme.
3. Mark off three columns in the space below the stars and rhyme.

4. Talk to your children about their wishes. Tell them that for every wish they have they can place a star in one of the columns.

5. Talk about the difference in wishes—some are hard to get; some can be attained through our own effort and keeping to a goal. Discuss the differences in the wishes they displayed. Underline the "star wishes" which are possible to reach.

6. As your children work toward the goal of their individual wishes, you (or they) can write in the column the various ways they helped reach their star—through their own effort.

27. My Responsible "Me"

Responsibility . . . is here defined as the ability to fulfill one's needs and to do so in a way that does not deprive others of the ability to fulfill their needs.

A responsible person also does that which gives him a feeling of self-worth and a feeling he is worthwhile to others.

William Glasser,
Reality Therapy

PURPOSE

To help children:

- focus on what their responsibilities are and understand that everyone has responsibilities.

- visualize their responsibilities and make them evident to others.

- experience a sense of worth as a result of accepting and fulfilling responsibilities.

SUGGESTED MATERIALS

For each child you will need:

- One sheet of poster board or card stock, approximately 12 x 18 inches

- Slips of scratch paper

- Colored gummed circles

- Marking pens with washable inks and/or water-soluble crayons or regular crayons

- Artist's compass

- Pencil, scissors

- Optional: photographs of children

Activity

1. Draw, or have your children draw, a stick figure representing a child on a large sheet of poster board. If you like, children's photographs may be used for faces on the stick figures. With the artist's compass, draw a handful of seven balloons, as shown in the illustration. Print the days of the week above

each balloon. Children may decorate their own charts with individual art work.

2. Have children decide what they will be responsible for each day of the week. Print these items on the slips of scratch paper along with the child's name. See that these are taped to the appropriate balloon.

3. At the end of each day, review with children their responsibilities. If they have followed through, they may attach a colored gummed circle to their balloon.

4. Have children check their balloons at the end of the week to see how often or how seldom they lived up to their responsibilities.

28. I Am All of These

To help the growing child to enlarge and deepen its vision and therefore its love, and at the same time to help it to become maker—maker of its own life as a whole human being with body, mind, heart, and will, and of its home, and of the larger family of the school, and eventually of the world family—that is the aim of education.

Gerald Vann
The Heart of Man

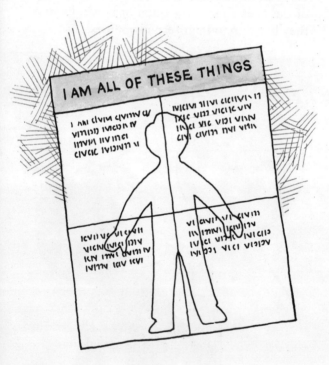

PURPOSE
To help children:

- realize that they are made up of body, thoughts, and feelings and that these unite to make up an individual.

- learn to accept their bodies, thoughts, and feelings and recognize that all of these may change from time to time.

- feel happy that they are the persons they are.

SUGGESTED MATERIALS
For yourself and each child you will need:

- One sheet of poster board or card stock approximately 12 x 18 inches

- Marking pens with washable inks and/or water-soluble crayons or regular crayons

- Old magazines or catalogs

- Double-stick tape, paste

- Photographs of children

- Pencil, ruler

Activity

1. At the top of the long end of the poster board, print the caption: I Am All of These Things.

2. Divide the poster board into four sections, marking off each section with a dotted line.

3. At the top of each section, print the following verses. Say or sing these to your children

from time to time and have them recite or sing
them with you.

I am toes and arms and legs and head;
I'm a body that must be clothed and fed;
I am all these as you can see;
I put them together—and they make me!

Once in a while I like to look
At grown-ups in a picture book.
I think of what I'd like to be;
I think and think—this, too, is me!

Sometimes I am happy, and sometimes
    I am sad.
Sometimes I am frightened, and sometimes
    I am glad.
I have so many feelings that sometimes
    you don't see,
I have so many feelings—and they are all
    a part of me.

I'm not just my body that runs and plays.
I'm not just my dreams that fill quiet days.
I'm not just the feelings that change in me.
I'm all of these things—and I'm glad
    I'm me!

4. As your children learn what each verse says,
   have them cut pictures from magazines or
   make drawings illustrating the first three
   sections: their body, their thoughts, their
   feelings. Let them paste a photograph of
   themselves in the last section.

5. Help them draw an outline of themselves
   over their entire poster and label this with
   their name.

A Concluding Note

There is something that can be found in one place. It is a great treasure, which may be called the fulfillment of existence. The place where the treasure may be found is the place on which one stands.

Martin Buber
To Hallow This Life

Twenty-eight activities have been given you to share with your children so that they may feel comfortable with themselves. These activities can also help *you* feel more alive and worthwhile as you share them with your children. The exercises emphasize helping your children feel at home with themselves (their own bodies, thoughts, and feelings), with their family, and with others in the wider world. They focus on a respect for individuality; an acceptance of and delight in one's own body, mind, and spirit; a recognition of the interdependence of human beings. Through these activities children should begin to find a deeper meaning in themselves and the world around them.

Through these activities you can learn more about your children and thus be better able to respond to their needs; you can show them you "listen" to them and thus help "reaffirm" themselves; you can give them an added sense of self-worth by stimulating the creative expression of themselves.

These experiences are designed to enhance a family atmosphere in which children feel valued and worthwhile, can become independent and learn to take charge of themselves, and are instilled with a sense of caring and responsibility. So, share these activities with your children and help them find and value the treasure that is themselves.

A Checklist—
The ABCs
of a Child's Needs

To help my children feel comfortable with
themselves, I will try to remember the ABCs of
their needs. Take a different letter for each day
and check your daily response: V=Okay; X=Not
Okay. I will give my child, I will allow my child,
I will help my child to know and to experience:

Achievement
Acceptance
Attention
Affection
Allowance for failure ☐

Belonging
Behavior models
Balance ☐

Care
Control
Cherishing
Creative play
Consistency
Curiosity ☐

Discipline
  Direction   ☐

Empathy
  Eagerness   ☐

Fairness
  Forgiveness   ☐

Goodness
  Gaiety   ☐

Honesty
  Happiness
  Honor   ☐

Independence
  Identity
  Individuality
  Imagination   ☐

Justice
  Joy   ☐

Kindness   ☐

Love
  Limits on behavior   ☐

Meaning in life
  Mental stimulation
  Models ☐

Nurturing newness ☐

Opportunity
  Openness ☐

Patience
  Play ☐

Questioning ☐

Responsibility
  Rootedness
  Relatedness ☐

Self-acceptance
  Satisfaction of needs
  Stability ☐

Trust
  Teaching ☐

Understanding
  Unity with others ☐

Value ☐

Worth
Watchfulness
Wonder ☐

Exploration
Example ☐

Youthfulness ☐

Zest ☐

If You Happen to Be a Teacher

In sharing these activities in a classroom situation, children learn to accept themselves and realize their own uniqueness, and to accept and appreciate the individual differences of others. More importantly, these activities help children *learn more about their overall similarities.* Children's relatedness with others will become more evident to them as they learn who they are as *individuals,* and also how *alike* one another they are. For the teacher, the result is a classroom environment with a comfortableness and understanding among students, an environment in which learning occurs more easily and effectively.

All children have a need for realizing their separate identities, and also a need for a sense of belonging and rootedness. They have a need for acceptance, affection, achievement, and a feeling of being significant to others and worthwhile. The 28 activities in this book can help children, individually and together, realize: "We're all like this. We are different, and yet we are the same."